A Beautiful Jigsaw

GW00469249

Antonia Kleopa

BookLeaf
Publishing

A Beautiful Jigsaw © 2022 Antonia Kleopa

All rights reserved.

Antonia Kleopa asserts the moral right to
be identified as author of this work.

Presentation by *BookLeaf Publishing*

Web: www.bookleafpub.com

E-mail: info@bookleafpub.com

ISBN: 9789357616706

First edition 2022

~For You, in all your strength, truth and glory~

ACKNOWLEDGEMENT

I want to thank God for the opportunities enabling me to enhance in my creative career, as well as guide and strengthen me in every aspect of my life.

To my partner, mi amor - you have continuously supported me and brought immense love and light into my world.

I also thank those around me who have supported me mentally, emotionally, and spiritually.

I want to thank those out there reading this - thank you for taking the time to hear my journey.

A big thank you to BookLeaf Publishing for this opportunity to get my work published!

Sending love out there, in our great universe.
Antonia x

PREFACE

Each poem in this collection represents specific moments in which were all important in each stage of my life to get me to where I am today. I have always searched for freedom, and what that meant to me. When I had been in the lowest moments where I had been experiencing mental health difficulties, I had never understood how much I needed to go to those painful places to get to the root of who I am and understand better; to heal and grow, understanding that it isn't linear.

I looked up to God, who guided me in my spiritual walk (which is ongoing!) and brought me back to my true self: who I always was and He destined me to be.
To help me understand what true freedom is. The art of letting go. Living in my truth. Going for my goals. Loving myself. Cultivating the life I want. In faith comes freedom, and anything is possible on this journey.

For those of you reading this collection, I hope that my words can reach a place inside you and help you see the light at the end of the tunnel. Because you are worth it. You are here for a reason. You hold the key to who you truly are. Nothing is impossible - even if the whole room looks dark - find the spark of light that ignites the place up again, that spark we all have within us.

And in the end...you will look through the telescope of your life and it will piece together like a beautiful jigsaw; exactly as it was meant to.

VOID

It feels...silent...
the silent pain
the silent words we never say
the silent love we wish to reach to another but
never do.
So we hide it all with a smile, a polite
"Thank you"

It knocks on my door.
I let it in as always.
A recurring nightmare and I want more.
I'm hunting
searching for something outside of me
because inside...

{inside I feel this void
this rotten root}

It shatters and breaks.
I'm steady in a high stake
of this prison of a place I call
"Home"

Wrapped up in a protective bed of cotton wool
away from the smoke

but
I relish it
swim in it
move in it
in this cold ecstasy.

Back to this vacant mentality
vacant insanity
which brings me further away from
freedom.

Maybe it's something we carry within us.
Dormant within us.
Anything outside feels almost foreign to me.
But I need to get out.

{if only I knew how}

OPERATION

To peel off a piece of my heart
guarded by the most protection.
This love
{shame it was never real}
only a
dark
toxic
infection.

Piece by piece I cut off to reveal to you:
open heart surgery
so you can see exactly what is inside my veins
pumping blood around the strain
you touch my whole
exterior
but won't tackle my operation
interior.

You got me:
end of project.

I close up.

Stitches back together – next?
Take out my stitches

but only creates these glitches
intruding on my chest
mentality impaired
patterns in despair
my heart says:
"No - wake up - you really should care"

Stomp your way into where my blood flows:
changing the beat of my rhythm
you change my mind –

{my mind isn't something you want though is
it?}

My heart bleeds in this contract of an operation
we call
"love"
flooding in tears
I wish I could refund
as I swim from the depths to reach above.

GLASS

Do you see it in my eyes at all?
That sweet smile I paint on to mask what lies
beneath my eyes.
A burning soul of passion yet
a denial glass gloss coating the scars of
loneliness
that have rooted a
home within me.

Feeding it with the voids of temporary attention
sexual aggression to keep me turned
on.
On - because feeling feels too hard at times so
I'm
off.
Gone.
     Switched
up.

When you touch my heart:
my soul;
my mind;
before my body...
the glass shatters
in this outbreak

of what feels like a prison of a place I call
"Home"

{home
sweet
scars}

Scars stay vacant clawing to the surface of my
thoughts
through this blind dance in the darkness
that is all too familiar to me.
I feed the steps with pumped up poison
to which my taste buds seek delight.
This bitter aftertaste wakes me through the night
to remind me about this flawed mentality in a
fright.
So tell me…

Do you see it in my eyes at all?

{unmasked}

GHOST

A passionate dinner.
Your tongue in twisting jealousies.
Hennessy:
you get drunk
off the touch of my hands.

Murmur whispers of delight in a language I
understand.
To my ears you speak truth
as we greet our
joys together
come together
love together.

{But}
I remember what you said
when you said you would
flight far
from this feeling
to not feel so...

~?~

You are a poison to love
because you felt it was

true:
you were falling for something
you are simply not used to.

RECYCLED

You.
Me.
Him.
Her.

We swirl in an incestuous whirlpool of
desire and pain;
living through the gain
we won from
one
the love we stole from
one
the hurt we adopt from
one
lean on
one.

Only to feed our own demons thirsty for blood
from a
cut
that I never even held the knife for

~?~

Unanswered questions hypocritically spoken on
the
tongue
that repeated your pattern in another
space
time
until you meet mine.

Mine is what brings
you to me
me to you
until I'm dispatched:
recycled to the next
staining them from the past figures of historical
partners
in which we swam together:
mixing the substances of
"love and hate"
only to duplicate into this
rebirth.

Only for him to ask me next:
"You're bleeding on me for a cut I never even
held the knife for?"
As this vicious infection continuously spirals;
immune to communication
immune to feeling
Immune to true love
immune to something...

real.

{I wish I could find the cure for this deadly virus
we spread to one another in a recycle of
hearts}

POISON

Wanting the black poison.
To swim in it
caress myself in it
inside and out
because it
feels
so
good.

{did the heartbreak feel as good?}

Growing in a mud unfed.
Mind unfed.
Heart unfed.
Hungry hearts.
Hungry eyes.

We never wined and dined
only confined in me to
transport me to
fly.
But in which direction?

~I cannot decide~

Wings clean of this black tar dictating my
direction
poisoning my growth from the seed that is sown
I cut off those branches
leaves hanging dry in the wind
as these wings are now
arching.

WILD

She moves through the world
collecting what she needs and
baring what she feels
unafraid to admit
she commits
to her flaws
as well as her
beauty.

A free spirit
and a wild heart.

JIGSAW

Shells:
defragmented pieces of what is now rusted gold.
Painted from the patterns of childhood
which we seek to keep buffered and shining
into adulthood by
another's hands.

We choreograph a dance together
deemed
{too damaged}
for a performance
in front of the reality check
of an audience named
"the help"

One missed step and you won't need them no
more
no longer the buffer to keep your
broken
pieces from shining
born out of a liquid substance
it covers our damages with a gloss
a sugar coat of glow
to cover the eruption
beneath

{the cry out for love}

Affection.
Something deeper than mere
attention of a
look
but instead…

something to fit the missing pieces
you were hungry to gain
from growing up
until you meet an equivalent.

You feed one another
fixing
p i e c i n g
the missing fragments
of what smells familiar to
you.

{not foreign - but home}

Home.
To remind you
what this eruption is telling you…
that you've suppressed for far too long.

Only to meet your perfect match

in the jigsaw that you find to
bring
you
back to
you
but now

dancing alone.

FREE

Plane jumping
soul thumping
creating a world that I'm
hunting
existing in me to fill the
void.

Every
city
every
new drink
every
meal
that I eat
I drink
I swallow
injecting the passions
rid of my sorrows.

~onset emotion: anxiety~

Yet the moment we realise how
we were never in control anyway
we then wish to trade this in for a
mind state of...

freedom
where nothing else exists except

~infinity~

infinite freedom equates to infinite choice.

What I have seen and
will see
one day I
will live out
to the extent that my heart
pumps
so my soul doesn't feel
drought.

Home is that freedom that this plane provides
my only wish is to be

free

have freedom to

fly.

SORRY

'Sorry' is a word
as foreign as a new language to my tongue.
'Sorry' is a word
I have never introduced
when my mind allowed me to reach for a more
bittersweet toxicity.
Toxins inside trying to multiply
but I only wish to sanctify
these cells into a
pure
apology.

An apology to me:
I to I
yet eyes not across to one another
{pillow talking melodies}
but eyes that are
mine.
The relation and dedication I have needed
to connect with myself
yet my mouth cannot seem to grasp for the word
'Sorry'

Let me forgive myself:

for stepping over my own heart to explore your
bloodline instead of
mine.

Let me forgive myself:

for trying to become more than I already am just
so I can entertain you like a shrine.

Let me forgive myself:

for never having realised my own potential to
love and be loved in all that I already am.

Let me forgive myself:

For all the times I had put up an armour as a
protection from
feeling.

And let me forgive myself for:
letting you in
letting you disrupt my
healing;
something I knew but ignored.

{A perfect contradiction to my story}

Unapologetic in

trusting
loving
sharing
caring

I will never apologise for wanting more out of
another
who has merely met himself as far as he has
allowed.

I will not be your
teacher
or
student
or
even your project
to fill a lonely night away from the crowd.

But I am sorry yes – to myself.
for thinking I was never good enough.

Too unlovable; yet too loving.
Too deep; yet too shallow.
Too hard; yet too easy.
Too perfect; yet too broken.

I will not allow any scar that is
buried within the
depths of me

to stay vacant enough to blur
my heart's vision
my soul
my understanding
instead I wish them to
flourish into something
more beautiful than they already are
to touch those soft petals that give me
the simple truth that is...
It was always about me:

{I was always enough all along}

HOPE

Space.
Unknown.
Until I saw glimpses of

s c a t t e r e d stars

they called out to me as
flickers of hope.
But not only did they shine
but stayed
vacant in the sky
to remind me that
whilst bathing in this element of mine
I will find
light where dark lives
and always a way to look up to
Breathe.
Breathe from the surface.
I realise that just like stars…

{Hope is always infinite}

BLOOM

Bloom again.

For the new season
the new version of
You.

Every tear that I release
sheds a tiny part of me
yet somehow that same

             d

             r

             o

             p

is the water
to feed
a great part of my
growth.

~a recycle of who you are becoming~

Shedding old petals
for new ones to
grow.

Let enthusiasm bind as your new normality

to shred that signature that you first signed

~?~

it was only a condition to steal away from your
time...
so create a new contract
from yourself to yourself
and sign it in
BOLD
with your choices
as you enter a new page

{create your own vision}
{transform above the norm}

THE MOON'S PERSPECTIVE

~The view from space~

Everything below seems so minuscule
like menial conversations
tragically overtaking meaningful ones
in a race against the purity of
truth and understanding;
misusing the presence of our third eye

'Perception beyond ordinary sight'
as the lack of stepping outside of the frame
seems apparent -
so the comfortability lies in becoming the
knitting and weaving within the
"picturesque" view inside.

And so the phases take their place.
~the Moon's perspective~

LAY

Laying with you wondering...
is this real or a
dream?

When my demons have manipulated me
otherwise
to convince me that I'm forbidden from
goodness of a feeling:
yet your embrace creates a
warmth underneath my skin that crawls to
e v e r y
crevice
of my body as this leading light -
bright enough to keep me constant
shutting out the darkness that
you label as
expired
as a means of protection.

You - are - this affection - in every direction...
I stay
close enough to hear your
body beat
like a jigsaw piece -
ourmindtracksmeet

as I lay with you wondering...
it isn't a dream.

This is real.
This is written.

{the pure intimacy of simply being understood}

EXIST

Existing:
a product of exiting the last door
I closed
a receipt of all the scars
imposed
wondering how did I get here
(?)
social deconstruction
self decomposition
compartmentalising thoughts
coexisting with the old and the new
as I hold the remote to switch between the
two
I feel a sense of a
twitch
a
glitch
in the system claiming this is something I'm not
accustomed to but -
belong to.

Trailing through this path
{there is a sweat to this walk}
as the empty remains of salt appear
utilising it to rub my wounds

to reveal hence -
heal
revealing all what is here and ahead
spotting myself as I sit upon the tree
that tells me

. . .

There is no tomorrow without the current of
today.

Exist.

DEBRIS

When all is
spoken with the
tongue
viewed through the
eyes
what is left?

Debris of this . . . (?)

Least to say
disaster
struck as it was
meant to.
Optimism has taken a break for
trust to be tested
into these depths of
dry waters
without the knowing of the
result.

All is in hands higher than any of us could
grasp
s c a t t e r e d debris sinks into my skin;
forming scars as they
melt...

their way in
yet my heart stays guarded
rinsed of toxins as they act like burglars
yet nobody can steal me from my
focus above.

~God knows me~

EXPOSED

Plans are only mere drops of ink
to be carried onto the paper of
your story
yet not always
fleshed out
into the original sense you
wrote out
forgetting the script is already written for
you.

To just
be - not act -
don't allow solidified ideas to
engrave rocks which are attached to
chains
pulling at the
strain
of what exposes your
pain
it belongs in the now
{deal with it don't dilute}
-it'll only pollute-
and digress you from the next

~Chapter~

You are the core actor
which God intends to move you
from behind those curtains to...
centre stage.

~Trust is the new wage~

PASSION CRY

Like an overflowing glass
I've got to ask myself:
Is it
half e m p t y or half-full?
Pass
that question on
and let it dampen my
mind
I plan to leave it all
behind
because I'm not blind to
see
that my passion is crying to see
me
I can hear it's wanting to be
heard
I can feel it's wanting to be
felt
as the vision still stands
souring out like a
bird.

~mantra: do what you love and that is all~

HIM

Saw you from afar.

Your solitude ignited my own...
the room you cook the tracks of your soul in;
red
blue
yellow
lights as we dance the night away
to a new town

{the opening of the world for me}

to grow
to understand
to let go

bodies of warmth
delve into dreams
stories to share
your words are music to my ears
the touch upon intimacy cravings -
1am.

~I saw the crescent whilst you saw the whole of
the moon~

Each creative moment adds to the flowing river
of your music;
the harmonic connection between you and the
world
so play the melody of your being
as we hear the
colours of your soul.

Your words influence my tongue
as we speak the same language
of affection.

Morning.
Sunshine.
Coffee.
And you.

Our adventure -
an ongoing excavation I'm built to dive deep for
I see how a lust for wander makes you
speak
and
move
soulfully
as it fills me up...

now I see
how you see

and
you...
see me.

Your grounding foundations of love:
my person.

A never-ending story:
our spirits connect.

Every moment is magical with you.

HUMAN

All we yearn for is the human experience.

To be
shared
cared
and
dared to be
bare
at the core
of it's rawness
because vulnerability
shouldn't cost any
price
when you're heart isn't willing to
suffice
to any lack of understanding.

Being in your purest form
is the least we owe ourselves.

~spirits connect~

PRAYER

Dear Lord,

Your comfort gives me a light in every way
especially through the darker days.

You are the power source to the torch that I hold
to guide me through the tunnel of my
circumstances however narrow or wide.

The truth to ground me in my innermost
authentic parts of myself
who you know me to be.

You eradicate fear and replace it with peace
anxiety has no place here.

You are hope and love in the world and the
heavens:
eternity is you.

The teacher of my dreams
you heal those parts of me in my sleep.

You pick me up and isolate me
to grow.

The creator of life:
only through you.

♡

Lord,
I grasp onto the word
to hold and to keep
to live and to learn
I love you.
I am yours.
Always.

  . . .

Amen.

♡

9 789357 616706